FINANCE FUNDAMENTALS

MASTERING FINANCIAL MANAGEMENT FOR BUSINESS SUCCESS

DR. JAGADEESH PILLAI

Made with ♥ on the Notion Press Platform
www.notionpress.com

|| Dedicated to all wisdom seekers around the world ||

Contents

Contents

Prayer

"Om Bhadram Karnebhih Shrunuyaama DevaahBhadram Pashyemaakshabhiryajatraah SthirairangaistushtuvaamsastanoobhihVyashema Devahitam YadaayuhSwasti Na Indro VridhashravaahSwasti Nah Pooshaa VishwavedaahSwasti Nastaarkshyo ArishtanemihSwasti No Brihaspatir DadhaatuOm Shantih, Shantih, Shantih"

The literal meaning of this mantra is: OM. O Gods! Let us hear auspicious words from our ears. O reverent Gods! Let us behold propitious visions from our eyes, let our organs and body be stable, healthy, and strong. Let us do that which is pleasing to the gods in the life span allotted to us. May Indra, inscribed in the scriptures, bring us fortune! May Pushan, the knower of the world, grant us prosperity! May Trakshya, who vanquishes enemies, bestow us with blessings! May Brihaspati bring us success!
OM Peace, Peace, Peace.

About The Author

Dr. Jagadeesh Pillai is a renowned Guinness World Record holder, writer, and researcher hailing from Varanasi, also known as the abode of Lord Shiva. With a Ph.D. in Vedic Science and a range of creative ideas and achievements, he is a true polymath. He is the author of more than 100 books including Research Publications. Although his roots can be traced back to Kerala, the people of Varanasi hold him in high regard and affectionately consider him one of their own.

In 1998, Dr. Pillai was offered a job at Banaras Hindu University, but he left the position after only two months to pursue greater goals in life. He believed that in order to study Indian scriptures and engage in other creative endeavours, he needed to retire from the daily grind of working solely for money at a young age.

He started an export business from scratch, using the knowledge he had gained from a previous job in the industry. His intelligence and unique approach to business led to great success in a short period of time, earning him more in just a decade and a half than he would have in a lifetime working in a government job. Upon the passing of Dr. APJ Abdul Kalam, Dr. Pillai decided to leave the business and dedicate himself to reading, studying, researching, and experimenting.

During his tenure in the export business, Dr. Pillai traveled to over 16 countries, gaining valuable insight and experiencing the world and life in detail.

Dr. Pillai has achieved four Guinness World Records in the following subjects:

"Script to Screen" - In this record, Dr. Pillai produced and directed an animation film within the shortest time possible, breaking the previous record set by Canadians. He has also received numerous national and international awards and recognitions for this achievement.

Longest Line of Postcards - For this record, Dr. Pillai created a line of 16,300 postcards on the occasion of the 163rd anniversary of Indian Postal Day. The event also included a questionnaire about the Indian flag.

Largest Poster Awareness Campaign - Dr. Pillai designed an awareness campaign on the subject of "Beti Bachao - Beti Padhao" (Save the Girl Child - Educate the Girl Child) to achieve this record.

Largest Envelope - In tribute to the Indian Prime Minister's "Make in India" initiative, Dr. Pillai created a 4000 square meter envelope using waste paper to achieve this record.

Attempted - **70000 Candles on a 210 kg Cake** - To celebrate the 70th Indian Independence Day, Dr. Pillai attempted to light 70,000 candles on a 210 kg cake, which was recorded in World Records India.

Attempted - **Documentary on Dhamek Stupa of Sarnath in 17 Languages** - Dr. Pillai attempted to create a documentary on the Dhamek Stupa of Sarnath, dubbing it in 17 different languages. The result of this attempt is currently awaiting confirmation from the Guinness World Records.

Dr. Pillai is skilled in teaching the Bhagavad Gita, a Hindu scripture, and is popular among young people. He has helped many young people improve their lives through his motivational teachings.

In addition to teaching, he has composed and sung numerous Sanskrit Bhajans and patriotic songs.

He has also written and directed several short films and documentaries for awareness campaigns, and has volunteered with the police in both UP and Kerala to spread awareness about various issues through videos and photography.

Incredibly, he has produced and directed over 100 documentaries about the city of Varanasi, all on his own.

He has also helped and guided more than 25 boys and girls to achieve world records through creative and innovative methods. He is a multifaceted person who uses his intellect and the blessings given to him by God to excel in various areas. He is both a teacher and a student, always learning and teaching, and is able to master any subject he comes across.

He is a selfless social activist and motivational speaker who has overcome struggles and failures to become a successful and enthusiastic individual with a rich life experience.

In addition to his work with the Bhagavad Gita, he is also

an efficient Tarot card reader, Astro-Vastu consultant, and a talented singer and composer. He has sung the entire Ram Charita Manas and Bhagavad Gita in his own compositions, and has sung the phrase "Lokah Samastha Sukhino Bhavantu" in 50 different languages. He is currently working on a detailed and scientific study of Vedas, Upanishads, Puranas, and the Bhagavad Gita. He has also composed and sung the Hanuman Chalisa and Gayatri Mantra in 108 and 1008 different compositions, respectively.

Awards - Four Times Guinness World Records, Winner of Mahatma Gandhi Vishwa Shanti Puraskar, Mahatma Gandhi Global Peace Ambassador, Kashi Ratna Award, Dr. APJ Abdul Kalam Motivational Person of the Year 2017, Mother Teresa Award, Indira Gandhi Priyadarshini Award, Bharat Vikas Ratna Award, Udyog Ratna Award, Vigyan Prasar Award, Poorvanchal Ratn Samman.

Preface

"Finance Fundamentals: Mastering Financial Management for Business Success" is an essential guide for anyone looking to gain a solid understanding of financial management and how it can be used to drive business success. Whether you are an entrepreneur, a manager, or an executive, this book will provide you with the knowledge and skills you need to make informed financial decisions and achieve your goals.

Through clear explanations and real-world examples, this book covers the key concepts and tools of financial management, including financial analysis, budgeting, forecasting, and investment evaluation. It also explores the broader context of financial management, including the role of finance in strategic decision-making and the impact of economic and regulatory factors on financial performance.

With a focus on practical application, this book is designed to help you develop the skills and knowledge you need to succeed in today's fast-paced business environment. Whether you are looking to start your own business, manage a team, or take your career to the next level, this book will provide you with the tools and insights you need to succeed.

I hope that this book will be of great value to you and that it will help you to achieve your goals and reach your full potential in the world of finance and business.

CHAPTER ONE

Introduction to Corporate Finance

With the right guidance and knowledge, mastering financial management for business success is achievable.

In this chapter, we will explore the basics of corporate finance and how it can be used to help businesses succeed. We will look at the different types of financial instruments, the importance of budgeting and forecasting, and the role of financial analysis in decision-making.

At the core of corporate finance is the concept of capital structure. This is the mix of debt and equity that a company uses to finance its operations. Different types of debt and equity instruments can be used to finance a business, such as bonds, stocks, and loans. Understanding the different types of instruments and how they work is essential for any business.

Budgeting and forecasting are also important components of corporate finance. By creating a budget and forecasting future cash flows, businesses can better manage their finances and make informed decisions. Financial analysis is also a key part of corporate finance. By analyzing financial statements, businesses can identify areas of improvement and make better decisions.

Finally, corporate finance is about more than just numbers. It is also about understanding the risks and rewards associated with different financial instruments and making decisions that are in the best interest of the business. By understanding the fundamentals of corporate finance, businesses can make better decisions and increase their chances of success.

Corporate finance is an essential part of any business. By understanding the basics of corporate finance, businesses can make better decisions and increase their chances of success. With the right guidance and knowledge, mastering financial management for business success is achievable.

CHAPTER TWO

Financial Statements and Analysis

Financial statements and analysis are essential components of business management. They provide a comprehensive overview of a company's financial health and performance, allowing managers to make informed decisions about the future of their business.

Financial statements provide a snapshot of a company's financial position at a given point in time. They include the balance sheet, income statement, and cash flow statement. The balance sheet shows the company's assets, liabilities, and equity. The income statement shows the company's revenues and expenses. The cash flow statement shows the company's cash inflows and outflows.

Analysis of financial statements is a critical part of business management. It helps managers identify trends, assess risk, and make informed decisions about the future of their business. Financial analysis involves comparing financial statements over time, analyzing ratios, and evaluating the company's performance relative to its peers.

Financial statements and analysis are essential tools for business management. They provide a comprehensive overview of a company's financial health and performance, allowing managers to make informed decisions about the future of their business. By analyzing financial statements, managers can identify trends, assess risk, and make informed decisions about the future of their business. This helps them to maximize profits, minimize losses, and ensure the long-term success of their company.

CHAPTER THREE

Time Value of Money

Time value of money is an essential concept in business management. It is the idea that money available at the present time is worth more than the same amount in the future due to its potential earning capacity. This concept is used to evaluate investments, determine the present value of future cash flows, and compare the cost of money over time.

Businesses use the time value of money to make decisions about investments, capital budgeting, and financing. For example, when considering a new project, a business must decide whether the expected return on the investment is worth the cost of the capital. The time value of money helps to determine the present value of the expected future cash flows, which can then be compared to the cost of the capital. This helps the business to decide whether the project is worth pursuing.

The time value of money is also used to compare the cost of money over time. For example, when deciding between two financing options, a business can use the time value of money to compare the cost of borrowing money now versus later. This helps the business to determine which option is more cost-effective.

The time value of money is an essential concept in business management. It is used to evaluate investments, determine the present value of future cash flows, and compare the cost of money over time. By understanding and utilizing the time value of money, businesses can make informed decisions about investments, capital budgeting, and financing.

CHAPTER FOUR

Capital Budgeting

Capital budgeting is an essential part of business management. It is the process of analyzing and evaluating potential investments to determine whether they are worth pursuing. Capital budgeting involves assessing the costs and benefits of a proposed investment, and then making a decision about whether to proceed with the project.

The capital budgeting process begins with an analysis of the potential investment. This includes an assessment of the expected costs and benefits of the project, as well as an evaluation of the risks associated with it. The analysis should also consider the impact of the investment on the company's overall financial position. Once the analysis is complete, the decision-makers must decide whether the investment is worth pursuing.

The capital budgeting process is an important part of business management because it helps to ensure that investments are made wisely. By carefully evaluating potential investments, companies can avoid costly mistakes and ensure that their resources are used in the most efficient manner. Additionally, capital budgeting can help to identify opportunities for growth and expansion.

When making a decision about whether to pursue a potential investment, it is important to consider the long-term implications. Companies should consider the potential returns on the investment, as well as the potential risks. Additionally, companies should consider the impact of the investment on the company's overall financial position. By carefully evaluating potential investments, companies can make informed decisions that will help them to maximize their returns and minimize their risks.

Capital budgeting is an essential part of business management. It helps to ensure that investments are made wisely and that resources are used in the most efficient manner. By carefully evaluating potential investments, companies can make informed decisions that will help them to maximize their returns and minimize their risks.

CHAPTER FIVE

Risk and Return

Risk and return are two of the most important concepts in business management. Risk is the potential for loss or gain associated with any investment or venture, while return is the expected gain or loss from an investment. Understanding the relationship between risk and return is essential for any business manager, as it helps them make informed decisions about investments and other business activities.

Risk and return are inextricably linked. Generally, the higher the risk associated with an investment, the higher the potential return. Conversely, the lower the risk, the lower the potential return. This is known as the risk-return tradeoff. Business managers must weigh the potential risks and rewards of any investment or venture before making a decision.

When assessing risk and return, business managers must consider a variety of factors. These include the expected rate of return, the volatility of the investment, the liquidity of the investment, and the time horizon of the investment. Additionally, business managers must consider the risk tolerance of the company and its stakeholders.

Business managers must also consider the various types of risk associated with an investment. These include market risk, liquidity risk, credit risk, and operational risk. Market risk is the risk of losses due to changes in the market, while liquidity risk is the risk of losses due to a lack of liquidity. Credit risk is the risk of losses due to a borrower's inability to repay a loan, while operational risk is the risk of losses due to operational errors or mismanagement.

Ultimately, business managers must understand the relationship between risk and return in order to make informed decisions about investments and other business activities. By assessing the various risks and rewards associated with an investment, business managers can make decisions that maximize returns while minimizing risks. This is essential for any successful business.

CHAPTER SIX

Cost of Capital

Cost of capital is an important concept in business management. It is the rate of return that a company must earn on its investments in order to satisfy its investors and creditors. The cost of capital is determined by the amount of risk associated with the investment and the expected return. It is important for businesses to understand the cost of capital in order to make informed decisions about investments and to ensure that they are able to generate sufficient returns to meet their financial obligations.

The cost of capital is determined by a variety of factors, including the company's credit rating, the current market conditions, and the expected return on the investment. Companies must consider the cost of capital when making decisions about investments, as it can have a significant impact on the profitability of the business. For example, if a company invests in a project with a higher cost of capital, it may not be able to generate sufficient returns to cover its costs.

In addition to the cost of capital, businesses must also consider the cost of debt and equity when making investment decisions. Debt is typically more expensive than equity, as it carries a higher risk of default. Equity, on the other hand, is typically less expensive, as it carries less risk. Companies must carefully weigh the cost of debt and equity when making investment decisions, as the cost of capital can have a significant impact on the profitability of the business.

When making investment decisions, businesses must also consider the cost of capital in relation to the expected return. Companies must ensure that the expected return is sufficient to cover the cost of capital, as this will ensure that the investment is profitable. Companies must also consider the risk associated with the investment, as this will determine the cost of capital.

Cost of capital is an important concept in business management. It is the rate of return that a company must earn on its investments in order to satisfy its investors and creditors. Companies must carefully consider the cost of capital, debt, and equity when making investment decisions.

CHAPTER SEVEN

Long-term Financing

Long-term financing is an important part of business management. It is the process of obtaining capital for a company's operations over a period of time that is longer than one year. Long-term financing can come from a variety of sources, such as banks, venture capitalists, and government grants.

When it comes to long-term financing, businesses must consider the cost of the capital, the terms of the loan, and the potential risks associated with the loan. The cost of the capital is the amount of money that must be paid back to the lender, plus any interest or fees associated with the loan. The terms of the loan are the length of time the loan is for, the repayment schedule, and any other conditions that must be met. Finally, businesses must consider the potential risks associated with the loan, such as the possibility of defaulting on the loan or the lender not being able to recover the money.

Businesses must also consider the benefits of long-term financing. Long-term financing can provide businesses with the capital they need to expand their operations, purchase new equipment, or hire additional staff. It can also provide businesses with the flexibility to adjust their operations as needed. Additionally, long-term financing can help businesses build their credit rating, which can be beneficial when seeking additional financing in the future.

Long-term financing is an important part of business management. It can provide businesses with the capital they need to grow and expand, while also providing them with the flexibility to adjust their operations as needed. However, businesses must consider the cost of the capital, the terms of the loan, and the potential risks associated with the loan before making a decision. By carefully weighing the pros and cons of long-term financing, businesses can make an informed decision that will help them achieve their goals.

CHAPTER EIGHT

Working Capital Management

Working capital management is an essential component of business management. It involves the efficient use of resources to ensure that a company has enough liquidity to meet its short-term obligations. Working capital management is a critical part of any business's financial strategy, as it helps to ensure that the company has enough cash on hand to cover its expenses and pay its bills.

The primary goal of working capital management is to maintain a balance between a company's short-term assets and liabilities. This balance is necessary to ensure that the company has enough liquidity to meet its short-term obligations. To achieve this balance, a company must carefully manage its current assets and liabilities. This includes managing cash, accounts receivable, inventory, and accounts payable.

Cash management is an important part of working capital management. Companies must ensure that they have enough cash on hand to cover their short-term obligations. This includes paying bills, making payroll, and purchasing inventory. Companies must also manage their accounts receivable and accounts payable to ensure that they are collecting payments from customers and paying their suppliers on time.

Inventory management is also an important part of working capital management. Companies must ensure that they have enough inventory on hand to meet customer demand. This includes managing the quantity and quality of inventory, as well as the timing of inventory purchases. Companies must also manage their inventory levels to ensure that they are not overstocked or understocked.

Finally, companies must manage their accounts payable and accounts receivable to ensure that they are collecting payments from customers and paying their suppliers on time. This includes managing the timing of payments, as well as the terms of payment. Companies must also ensure that they are not over-extending themselves financially by taking on too much debt.

Working capital management is a critical component of business operations. It requires the judicious utilization of resources to guarantee that a company has sufficient liquidity to fulfill its short-term commitments. Companies must vigilantly manage their cash, accounts receivable, and inventory to ensure that they have enough working capital to cover their expenses and remain profitable. By properly managing their working capital, businesses can ensure that they have the resources necessary to meet their financial obligations and remain competitive in the marketplace.

CHAPTER NINE

Financial Markets and Institutions

Financial markets and institutions play a critical role in business management. They provide the necessary capital for businesses to grow and expand, as well as the liquidity to facilitate transactions. Financial markets are the places where buyers and sellers of financial instruments, such as stocks, bonds, and derivatives, come together to trade. Financial institutions, such as banks, investment firms, and insurance companies, provide the necessary services and products to facilitate these transactions.

Financial markets and institutions are essential for businesses to access capital and liquidity. They provide the necessary capital for businesses to expand and grow, as well as the liquidity to facilitate transactions. For example, businesses can access capital through the stock market by issuing shares of their company. They can also access liquidity through the bond market by issuing debt instruments. Additionally, businesses can access liquidity through the derivatives market by trading futures and options.

Financial institutions provide the necessary services and products to facilitate these transactions. Banks provide loans and other financial services, such as checking and savings accounts. Investment firms provide advice and services related to investments, such as portfolio management and stock trading. Insurance companies provide insurance products, such as life insurance and health insurance.

Financial markets and institutions are essential for businesses to access capital and liquidity. They provide the necessary capital for businesses to expand and grow, as well as the liquidity to facilitate transactions. By understanding the role of financial markets and institutions in business management, businesses can make informed decisions about how to access capital and liquidity. This can help them to maximize their growth potential and increase their profitability.

CHAPTER TEN

Investment Analysis and Portfolio Management

Investment analysis and portfolio management are essential components of business management. They involve the evaluation of potential investments and the selection of the most suitable ones for a company's portfolio. Investment analysis involves the assessment of the risk and return of potential investments, while portfolio management involves the selection and management of investments to achieve the desired objectives.

Investment analysis requires a thorough understanding of the financial markets and the ability to identify and analyze the various factors that influence the performance of investments. This includes an understanding of the macroeconomic environment, the industry and sector dynamics, and the financial and operational performance of the companies in which investments are made. Investment analysis also requires an understanding of the various financial instruments available and the ability to assess their suitability for a particular portfolio.

Portfolio management involves the selection and management of investments to achieve the desired objectives. This includes the selection of the most suitable investments, the allocation of capital to those investments, and the monitoring of the performance of the investments. Portfolio management also involves the management of risk, including the identification and management of potential risks associated with investments.

Investment analysis and portfolio management are essential components of business management. They require a thorough understanding of the financial markets and the ability to identify and analyze the various factors that influence the performance of investments. Furthermore, portfolio management involves the selection and management of investments to achieve the desired objectives, as well as the management of risk. By utilizing these tools, businesses can maximize their returns and minimize their risks, allowing them to achieve their financial goals.

CHAPTER ELEVEN

International Finance

International finance is an integral part of business management. It involves the management of money and other financial assets across international borders. It is a complex field that requires a deep understanding of global markets, economic trends, and financial instruments.

The global economy is constantly changing, and international finance is a key factor in helping businesses stay competitive. Companies must be able to identify and capitalize on opportunities in foreign markets, while also managing risks associated with currency fluctuations, political instability, and other factors.

International finance is a complex and ever-evolving field. It requires a comprehensive understanding of global markets, economic trends, and financial instruments. Companies must be able to identify and capitalize on opportunities in foreign markets, while also managing risks associated with currency fluctuations, political instability, and other factors.

In order to succeed in international finance, businesses must have a thorough understanding of the global economy and its various components. They must be able to analyze and interpret financial data, identify potential risks and opportunities, and develop strategies to maximize returns. Additionally, businesses must be able to effectively manage their finances across multiple countries and currencies.

International finance is a critical component of business management. It requires a deep understanding of global markets, economic trends, and financial instruments. Companies must be able to identify and capitalize on opportunities in foreign markets, while also managing risks associated with currency fluctuations, political instability, and other factors. By doing so, businesses can remain competitive in the global economy and maximize their returns.

CHAPTER TWELVE

Derivatives

Derivatives are financial instruments that derive their value from an underlying asset. They are used by businesses to manage risk, increase liquidity, and generate returns.

Derivatives can be used to hedge against market volatility, allowing businesses to protect their investments from sudden price changes. For example, a business may purchase a put option to protect against a decline in the price of a stock. This allows the business to limit its losses if the stock price falls.

Derivatives can also be used to increase liquidity. By entering into a futures contract, a business can lock in a price for a commodity or security, allowing it to buy or sell the asset at a predetermined price. This can help businesses manage cash flow and reduce the risk of holding illiquid assets.

Finally, derivatives can be used to generate returns. By taking a long or short position in a derivative, businesses can speculate on the direction of the underlying asset and potentially generate profits. For example, a business may purchase a call option to speculate on a rise in the price of a stock. If the stock price rises, the business can sell the option for a profit.

In conclusion, derivatives are powerful tools that can be used by businesses to manage risk, increase liquidity, and generate returns. By understanding how derivatives work and how they can be used, businesses can make informed decisions and maximize their profits.

CHAPTER THIRTEEN

Behavioural Finance

Behavioural finance is an important concept in business management. It is the study of how people make financial decisions and how those decisions are influenced by psychological, cognitive, and emotional factors. It is a relatively new field of study, but it has become increasingly important in recent years as businesses have become more complex and globalized.

Behavioural finance seeks to understand why people make certain financial decisions and how those decisions can be influenced by psychological, cognitive, and emotional factors. It looks at how people perceive risk, how they make decisions, and how they react to different financial situations. It also examines how people's behaviour can affect the performance of a business.

For example, behavioural finance can help businesses understand why people may be more likely to invest in certain stocks or why they may be more likely to take on more risk. It can also help businesses understand why people may be more likely to buy certain products or services. By understanding these factors, businesses can make better decisions and create more effective strategies.

Behavioural finance can also help businesses understand how people's behaviour can affect the performance of a business. For example, if people are more likely to take on more risk, then businesses may need to adjust their strategies to account for this. Similarly, if people are more likely to invest in certain stocks, then businesses may need to adjust their strategies to account for this as well.

Overall, behavioural finance is an important concept in business management. It helps businesses understand why people make certain financial decisions and how those decisions can be influenced by psychological, cognitive, and emotional factors. By understanding these factors, businesses can make better decisions and create more effective strategies.

CHAPTER FOURTEEN

Corporate Governance

Corporate governance is an essential component of business management. It is the system of rules, practices, and processes that a company follows to ensure that it is managed responsibly and ethically. Corporate governance is designed to protect the interests of shareholders, employees, customers, and other stakeholders.

At its core, corporate governance is about creating a framework for decision-making that is transparent, accountable, and fair. It is about creating a culture of trust and responsibility within the organization. It is also about ensuring that the company is compliant with all applicable laws and regulations.

The primary goal of corporate governance is to ensure that the company is managed in a way that maximizes shareholder value. This is done by ensuring that the company is run in an efficient and effective manner, and that the interests of all stakeholders are taken into account.

The board of directors is responsible for overseeing the company's corporate governance. They are responsible for setting the company's strategic direction, approving major decisions, and ensuring that the company is compliant with all applicable laws and regulations. The board of directors is also responsible for appointing the company's executive officers and monitoring their performance.

The board of directors is also responsible for setting the company's corporate governance policies. These policies should be designed to ensure that the company is managed in a way that is consistent with the company's values and objectives. The policies should also be designed to ensure that the company is compliant with all applicable laws and regulations.

In addition to the board of directors, corporate governance also involves other stakeholders such as shareholders, employees, customers, and other stakeholders. These stakeholders should be consulted and their views taken into account when making decisions.

Ultimately, corporate governance is about cultivating a culture of trust and accountability within the organization. It is about ensuring that the company is managed in a manner that optimizes shareholder value and considers the interests of all stakeholders. Additionally, it is about guaranteeing that the company is in compliance with all applicable laws and regulations.

CHAPTER FIFTEEN

Financial Distress and Bankruptcy

Financial distress and bankruptcy are two of the most common issues that businesses face in the world of business management. When a business is in financial distress, it is unable to meet its financial obligations and is in danger of becoming insolvent. Bankruptcy is the legal process that a business goes through when it is unable to pay its debts.

Financial distress and bankruptcy can have a devastating effect on a business. It can lead to the closure of the business, the loss of jobs, and the loss of investments. It can also have a negative impact on the business's reputation and credit rating.

The causes of financial distress and bankruptcy can vary from business to business. Poor management decisions, inadequate capitalization, and a lack of cash flow are all common causes. Other factors such as economic downturns, changes in the industry, and competition can also contribute to financial distress and bankruptcy.

Businesses can take steps to avoid financial distress and bankruptcy. Proper financial planning and budgeting are essential. Businesses should also ensure that they have adequate capitalization and cash flow. Additionally, businesses should be aware of the risks associated with their industry and take steps to mitigate them.

When a business is in financial distress, it is important to take action quickly. Businesses should seek professional advice and consider restructuring or refinancing options. In some cases, bankruptcy may be the only option.

Financial distress and bankruptcy can have a significant impact on a business. It is important for businesses to be aware of the risks and take steps to avoid them. With proper planning and budgeting, businesses can reduce the risk of financial distress and bankruptcy and ensure their long-term success.

CHAPTER SIXTEEN

Mergers and Acquisitions

Mergers and acquisitions are a common occurrence in the business world. They are a way for companies to expand their operations, increase their market share, and gain access to new resources. Mergers and acquisitions involve the combining of two or more companies into one entity, or the purchase of one company by another.

The process of mergers and acquisitions can be complex and time-consuming. It requires careful planning and consideration of the legal, financial, and operational implications of the transaction. Companies must consider the potential benefits and risks associated with the transaction, as well as the potential impact on their employees, customers, and shareholders.

Mergers and acquisitions can be beneficial for both companies involved. They can provide access to new markets, resources, and technologies, as well as increased efficiency and cost savings. They can also help companies to diversify their operations and reduce their risk.

However, there are also potential risks associated with mergers and acquisitions. Companies must consider the potential for cultural clashes, the impact on employees, and the potential for regulatory issues. Additionally, the process of integrating two companies can be difficult and costly.

In order to ensure a successful merger or acquisition, companies must carefully consider the potential benefits and risks associated with the transaction. They must also ensure that they have the necessary resources and expertise to manage the process. Companies should also consider the potential impact on their employees, customers, and shareholders.

Mergers and acquisitions are an important part of business management. They can provide companies with access to new markets, resources, and technologies, as well as increased efficiency and cost savings. However, they also come with potential risks and challenges that must be carefully considered. Companies must ensure that they have the necessary resources and expertise to manage the process and consider the potential impact on their employees, customers, and shareholders.

CHAPTER SEVENTEEN

Financial Planning and Control

Financial planning and control is an essential component of business management. It involves the development of strategies and processes to ensure that a company's financial resources are used in the most efficient and effective manner possible. This includes budgeting, forecasting, and analyzing financial data to make informed decisions about the company's financial future.

Financial planning and control is a complex process that requires careful consideration of a company's current and future financial needs. It involves analyzing the company's financial position, assessing its financial goals, and developing strategies to achieve those goals. This includes creating a budget, forecasting cash flow, and analyzing financial data to identify areas of potential risk and opportunity.

Financial planning and control also involves monitoring and evaluating the company's financial performance. This includes analyzing financial statements, tracking financial trends, and assessing the company's financial health. This helps to ensure that the company is meeting its financial goals and objectives.

Financial planning and control is a critical component of business management. It helps to ensure that a company's financial resources are used in the most efficient and effective manner possible. By analyzing financial data, creating budgets, and monitoring financial performance, companies can make informed decisions about their financial future and ensure that they are on track to meet their financial goals.

CHAPTER EIGHTEEN

Treasury Management

Treasury management is an essential component of business management. It involves the management of a company's financial resources, including cash flow, investments, and risk management. It is a complex process that requires careful planning and execution.

The primary goal of treasury management is to ensure that a company has sufficient funds to meet its short-term and long-term financial obligations. This includes managing cash flow, investing in short-term and long-term investments, and managing risk.

Cash flow management is the process of managing the company's cash flow. This includes monitoring cash inflows and outflows, as well as forecasting future cash flow needs. It is important to ensure that the company has sufficient funds to meet its short-term and long-term financial obligations.

Investment management is the process of managing the company's investments. This includes selecting the right investments, monitoring their performance, and making adjustments as needed. It is important to ensure that the company's investments are diversified and that they are generating a return that meets the company's goals.

Risk management is the process of managing the company's exposure to risk. This includes identifying potential risks, assessing their impact, and developing strategies to mitigate them. It is important to ensure that the company is adequately protected from potential risks.

Treasury management is a complex process that requires careful planning and execution. It is essential for a company to have a well-defined treasury management strategy in order to ensure that it has sufficient funds to meet its short-term and long-term financial obligations. It is also important to ensure that the company's investments are diversified and that they are generating a return that meets the company's goals. Additionally, it is important to ensure that the company is adequately protected from potential risks. By properly managing its financial resources, a company can ensure its long-term success.

CHAPTER NINETEEN

Financial Engineering

Financial engineering is an integral part of business management. It involves the use of financial instruments and strategies to create value and manage risk. Financial engineering is used to optimize the use of capital, manage liquidity, and reduce the cost of capital. It also helps to identify and exploit opportunities for growth and profitability.

Financial engineering is a complex process that requires a deep understanding of financial markets, instruments, and strategies. It involves the use of sophisticated mathematical models and techniques to analyze and forecast financial markets and to identify and exploit opportunities for value creation. Financial engineers must be able to identify and evaluate risks, develop strategies to mitigate them, and create value through the use of financial instruments.

Financial engineering is a critical component of business management. It helps to optimize the use of capital, manage liquidity, and reduce the cost of capital. It also helps to identify and exploit opportunities for growth and profitability. Financial engineering is a complex process that requires a deep understanding of financial markets, instruments, and strategies. By leveraging the power of financial engineering, businesses can create value, manage risk, and maximize returns.

CHAPTER TWENTY

Real Estate Finance

Real estate finance is an integral part of business management. It involves the acquisition, management, and disposal of real estate assets in order to maximize returns and minimize risks. Real estate finance is a complex field that requires a thorough understanding of the legal, financial, and economic aspects of the real estate market.

Real estate finance involves a variety of activities, including the acquisition of land, the development of properties, and the management of investments. It also involves the analysis of financial statements, the evaluation of potential investments, and the negotiation of financing terms. In addition, real estate finance involves the management of cash flows, the assessment of risk, and the development of strategies to maximize returns.

Real estate finance is a critical component of business management. It requires a comprehensive understanding of the legal, financial, and economic aspects of the real estate market. It also requires an understanding of the various financing options available, including traditional bank loans, private equity, and venture capital. Furthermore, real estate finance requires an understanding of the tax implications of investments, the impact of inflation, and the potential risks associated with investments.

Real estate finance is a complex field that requires a deep understanding of the legal, financial, and economic aspects of the real estate market. It is essential for business managers to have a comprehensive understanding of the various financing options available, the tax implications of investments, and the potential risks associated with investments. By having a thorough understanding of real estate finance, business managers can make informed decisions that will maximize returns and minimize risks.

CHAPTER TWENTY-ONE

Project Finance

Project finance is an important component of business management. It involves the use of financial instruments to fund a project, such as a new building, a bridge, or a new product. Project finance is a complex process that requires careful planning and analysis.

Project finance involves the use of debt and equity to fund a project. Debt is typically provided by banks or other financial institutions, while equity is provided by investors. The debt and equity are used to finance the project, and the returns are shared between the lenders and the investors.

Project finance also involves the use of financial instruments such as derivatives, swaps, and options. These instruments are used to manage the risk associated with the project. They can also be used to hedge against changes in the market or to take advantage of opportunities.

Project finance also involves the use of financial models to assess the viability of the project. These models are used to determine the expected returns, the risk associated with the project, and the cost of financing. The models are also used to determine the optimal capital structure for the project.

Project finance is a complex process that requires careful planning and analysis. It involves the use of financial instruments to fund a project, the use of financial models to assess the viability of the project, and the use of derivatives, swaps, and options to manage the risk associated with the project. By understanding the complexities of project finance, businesses can make informed decisions and maximize their returns.

CHAPTER TWENTY-TWO

Taxation

Taxation is an integral part of business management. It is essential for businesses to understand the various taxation laws and regulations in order to remain compliant and maximize their profits. Taxation can be a complex and daunting task, but with the right knowledge and strategies, businesses can effectively manage their taxes and ensure their financial success.

Taxation is a key factor in business management, as it affects the profitability of a business. It is important to understand the various types of taxes, such as income tax, sales tax, and property tax, and how they apply to a business. Additionally, businesses must be aware of the various deductions and credits available to them, as well as the different tax rates that apply to different types of income.

Businesses must also be aware of the various tax laws and regulations that apply to them. These laws and regulations can vary from state to state, and it is important for businesses to stay up to date on the latest changes. Additionally, businesses must be aware of the various tax incentives and deductions that are available to them, as well as the different filing requirements.

Finally, businesses must be aware of the various tax planning strategies that can help them minimize their tax liability. These strategies include deferring income, taking advantage of deductions and credits, and utilizing tax-advantaged investments. By understanding the various taxation laws and regulations, businesses can effectively manage their taxes and maximize their profits.

Taxation is an essential part of business management, and it is important for businesses to understand the various taxation laws and regulations in order to remain compliant and maximize their profits. With the right knowledge and strategies, businesses can effectively manage their taxes and ensure their financial success. By understanding the various taxation laws and regulations, businesses can take advantage of tax incentives and deductions, utilize tax-advantaged investments, and develop effective tax planning strategies to minimize their tax liability. With the right knowledge and strategies, businesses can effectively manage their taxes and ensure their financial success.

CHAPTER TWENTY-THREE

Credit Risk Management

Credit risk management is an essential component of business management. It involves the identification, assessment, and mitigation of risks associated with the use of credit. By understanding and managing credit risk, businesses can protect their financial assets and ensure their long-term success.

The first step in credit risk management is to identify the sources of credit risk. This includes assessing the creditworthiness of customers, suppliers, and other parties with whom the business has financial relationships. It also involves understanding the terms of credit agreements and the potential for default.

Once the sources of credit risk have been identified, the next step is to assess the risk. This involves analyzing the creditworthiness of customers and suppliers, as well as the terms of credit agreements. It also involves assessing the potential for default and the potential losses that could result from a default.

The final step in credit risk management is to mitigate the risk. This involves developing strategies to reduce the potential for default and to minimize the potential losses that could result from a default. Strategies may include setting credit limits, requiring collateral, and monitoring customer accounts.

By understanding and managing credit risk, businesses can protect their financial assets and ensure their long-term success. By taking the time to identify, assess, and mitigate credit risk, businesses can reduce their exposure to potential losses and create a more secure financial future.

CHAPTER TWENTY-FOUR

Financial Innovation and Fintech

Financial innovation and fintech have revolutionized the way businesses manage their finances. By leveraging the power of technology, businesses can now access a wide range of financial services that were previously unavailable. From automated payments to real-time analytics, fintech has enabled businesses to streamline their financial operations and make more informed decisions.

The emergence of fintech has enabled businesses to access a variety of financial services that were previously unavailable. From automated payments to real-time analytics, businesses can now access a wide range of financial services that can help them make more informed decisions. Additionally, fintech has enabled businesses to reduce costs associated with traditional financial services, such as banking fees and transaction costs.

Fintech has also enabled businesses to access new sources of capital. By leveraging the power of technology, businesses can now access alternative sources of financing, such as crowdfunding and peer-to-peer lending. This has enabled businesses to access capital that was previously unavailable to them, allowing them to expand their operations and pursue new opportunities.

Furthermore, fintech has enabled businesses to access a variety of financial services that can help them manage their finances more effectively. From automated payments to real-time analytics, businesses can now access a wide range of financial services that can help them make more informed decisions and manage their finances more efficiently.

Financial innovation and fintech have revolutionized the way businesses manage their finances. By leveraging the power of technology, businesses can now access a wide range of financial services that were previously unavailable. From automated payments to real-time analytics, fintech has enabled businesses to streamline their financial operations and make more informed decisions. Additionally, fintech has enabled businesses to access new sources of capital and manage their finances more effectively. As such, fintech has become an essential tool for businesses looking to stay competitive in today's rapidly changing financial landscape.

Other Books Of The Author

1. The Moments When I Met God
2. Kashiyile Theertha Pathangal
3. GURU GYAN VANI
4. Abhiprerak Gita
5. ASSI SE JAIN GHAT TAK
6. Hopelessness of Arjuna
7. The Soul and It's True Nature
8. Sense of Action (Karma)
9. Action through Wisdom
10. Action through Wisdom
11. THEORY AND PRACTICAL OF EVERY ACTION
12. LOGICAL UNDERSTANDING OF THE SUPREME
13. THE IMPERISHABLE SUPREME
14. Yatra Nishadraj se Hanuman Ghat Tak
15. Yatra Karnatak Ghat se Raja Ghat Tak
16. Yatra Pandey Ghat se Prayagraj Ghat Tak
17. Yatra Ranjendra Prasad Ghat se Dattatreya Ghat Tak
18. YaatraSindhiya Ghat se Gwaliar Ghat Tak
19. Yatra Mangala Gauri Ghat se Hanuman Gadhi Ghat Tak
20. Yatra Gaay Ghat Se Nishad Ghat Tak
21. MAA GANGA, GHATEN EVM UTSAV
22. Ganga Arti Dev Deepavali evam Any Utsav
23. Potentials of Digitalized India
24. VEDIC CONSCIOUSNESS
25. A Brief Introduction to Vedic Science
26. Kashi ke Barah Jyotirling
27. IMPACT OF MOTIVATION
28. Let's have a Milky Way Journey
29. Color Therapy in a Nutshell

30. Rigveda in a Nutshell
31. Yajurveda in a Nutshell
32. Samveda in a Nutshell
33. Atharva Veda in a Nutshell
34. Ayushman Bhava Ayurveda
35. Srimad Bhagavad Gita and Upanishad Connection
36. Srimad Bhagavad Gita - an attempt to summarize each chapter.
37. Facts and Impact of Nakshatra
38. Astro Gems - NAVARATNA
39. Ekadashi - A Concise Overview
40. A Concise View of Hanuman Chalisa
41. Inspirational Gita
42. Nakshatraranyam
43. Summary of 18 Mahapuranas
44. Synopsis of 18 Upa Puranas
45. Rigvediya Upanishads
46. Shukla Yajurvediya Upanishads
47. Krishna Yajurvediya Upanishads
48. Samavediya Upanishads
49. Atharvavediya Upanishads
50. The Seven Great Sages
51. From Rocket Scientist to President Dr. APJ Abdul Kalam
52. The Visionary's Voice - Quotes of Dr. APJ Abdul Kalam
53. The Wisdom of Swami Vivekananda: Insights and Inspiration from a Legendary Spiritual Teacher
54. Ayurvedic Remedies from the Garden
55. Sages and Seers
56. Rising Strong – Motivational Stories of Women
57. Beyond Flames -Mystery stories of Funeral Ghat Manikarnika
58. The Origins of Tulsi: A Look at the Mythological Roots of the Plant"

59. The Holistic Cow: A Look at the Physical, Spiritual, and Cultural Importance of Cows in India
60. Arts of Healing
61. Exploring the Divine
62. Understanding Five Elements
63. The Etymology of Ram
64. Symbols of India
65. Voice of Change (About Speeches of Great Men)
66. She Speaks (About Speeches of Great Women)
67. Patriotism on Celluloid – Brief About Patriotic Films
68. The Music of Motivation: A Brief Guide to Inspirational Film Songs
69. **Unlocking the Secrets of the Dashopanishads**
70. A Cultural Mosaic
71. Ancient Traditions, Modern Minds
72. Ecos of Ancient Wisdom
73. Beneath the Surface
74. From Temples to Ashrams
75. Sages of the Subcontinent
76. The Art of Healling (Ayurveda, Yoga & Naturopathy)
77. Indian Kitchen
78. The Festivals of India
79. The Indian Epics Retold
80. The Power of Mantras
81. The Indian River Ganges
82. The Indian Architecture
83. Rites of Passage
84. The Indian Silk Road
85. The Indian Literature
86. The Indian Villages
87. The Indian Folks & Crafts
88. The Way of Buddha
89. The Ramayan of Tulsidas

90. Astrological Remedies
91. The Secret Power of Motivation
92. Secret of Developing your Inner Strength
93. The Secret Path to Motivation
94. The Art and Secret of Positive Thinking
95. The Secrets of Practicing Ethical Living
96. Indian Art and Painting
97. The Indian Herbalism
98. Bharatanatyam to Kathak
99. Exploring India's Astrological Remedies
100. The Indian Festival of Flowers
101. Indian Handicrafts
102. The Splashes of Joy – India's Colour Festival
103. The Indian Science of Astrology
104. The Indian Mythology
105. Path to Enlightenment
106. The Indian Spirituality for Children
107. Aromas of India
108. The Secrets of Healthy Relationships
109. Ancestral Ties
110. The Indian Street Food
111. Discovering America
112. The Indian Textile
113. Listening to Motivational Speeches
114. Taste of India
115. A Cultural Journey through Indian Nuptials
116. Motivational Quote for Change
117. Secret Strategies for Making Money
118. Secrets to Cultivate a Positive Mindset
119. A Tapestry of Cultures: Exploring India from Kashmir to Kanyakumari
120. Achieving Your Dreams with Resilience: Secret Strategies for Overcoming Obstacles

121. Innovative Startups - 25 Startup Ideas to Spark Your Business Creativity
122. Export Management: Strategies for Global Success
123. Exporting from India - A Step by Step Guide
124. Finance Fundamentals: Mastering Financial Management for Business Success
125. Global Growth Strategies for International Business Development
126. Marketing Mastery: Unlocking the Secrets of Modern Marketing
127. Operations Mastery: Managing the Flow of Value in Business
128. Strategic Business Management: Navigating the Modern Business Landscape
129. Human Resource Management Strategies for Building and Managing a High Performance Team

Contact

DR. JAGADEESH PILLAI

MBA & PhD in Vedic Science

Four Times Guinness World Record Holder

Winner of Mahatma Gandhi Vishwa Shanti Puraskar and
Global Peace Ambassador

Gemology, Astro & Vastu Consultant - Spiritual Counselor

Consultant for designing World Record Ideas

Efficient Tarot Card Reader

9839093003

myrichindia@gmail.com

drjagadeeshpillai@facebook

drjagadeeshpillai@instagram
jagadeeshpillai@youtube

www. JAGADEESHPILLAI.com

|| LOKAHA SAMASTHAHA SUKHINO BHAVANTU ||

Printed by Libri Plureos GmbH in Hamburg,
Germany